ME TO MYSELF

REKHA ASHOK

I dedicate this book to:-

My parents, who instilled moral values in me.

Mrs Pratibha Prakash, my mentor who saw the best in me.

Mr Anil Neendakara, who inspired me into penning down my emotions.

And for all those who encouraged me to fly towards my dreams.

LET'S SOAR

Contents

Preface *vii*

Acknowledgements *ix*

Part 1

1. Me To Myself 3
2. Poetry To Me... 4
3. Teacher-student Bond 5
4. My Mom My Strength 6
5. Growing Wiser 8
6. I Wish..... 10
7. Arachnophobia 11
8. Adam's Ale 12
9. Mighty Night 14
10. Smile 15
11. Reading Gives You Wings 16
12. Family Wedding 17
13. Piscean 19
14. Working In A School 20
15. True Relations 21
16. Greenery 22
17. Wrath 23
18. Success 24
19. Harmony 25
20. Words Of Wisdom 27

Preface

In 'ME and MYSELF', my first anthology, I have shared the strange ways how life teaches one the different aspects of emotions and how to make better sense of life's important matters. I uphold human values and promote mutual respect which is reflected in my poetry compilation. In my book, I discuss both my experiences and how they changed me.

I wish to explore with my ears sharp and eyes keen,

I face the unknown with faith,that's how I have been.

Acknowledgements

As much as I would just love to take all the credit for this book, there are a lot of people who had a hand in making this dream come true.

Thank you, divine spirit, for giving me this insight and writing skill.

I would like to acknowkedge the extraordinary debt I owe to my parents who always believed in me.

Most of all I want to thank my children and students who shower me with so much love and respect. They have taught me a lot too. I also wish to thank my family, my mentors and my colleagues for their invaluable support.

1. ME TO MYSELF

I let my heart accept
the imperfect version of myself.
I am a queen because
I know how to rule myself.
The wisest thing I can do
is to be on my own side.
I know I am not alone,
I have myself for aide.
I take pride in being authentic
and the uniqueness I own.
I am still young and
every day I want to learn on.
I celebrate my self confidence
that gives me a high.
And how I feel inside
reflects in my eye.
I'm in the process
of discovering myself,
And all the way trying
to be the best version of myself.

2. POETRY TO ME...

Poetry to me is not a shopping list
or a bare pretension,
Poetry is a political action for
the faith and lyrical invention.
Poetry is to make telling
the truth lyrical and possible,
Poetry is language of your feelings
that makes it audible.
Poetry is a tool to build
a long lasting relationship,
Poetry is a way of speaking
and listening to companionship.
Poetry is song of the
soul without music,
Poetry is imaginative awareness
that's always therapeutic.
And that's what poetry is to me!!!

3. TEACHER-STUDENT BOND

Ideas and words are my knowledge,
that I toss like leaves into the air.
I watch as they float around
the many ear to bear.
I rejoice to see my words being caught,
And they inspire me with the queries they have got.
I paint their minds and guide their thoughts,
And share their success and advise their faults.
I stimulate the minds with knowledge and truth,
And see their path brighten to lead the youth.
Only mutual respect build a special place in their heart,
that would motivate them to get their start.
I love teaching them how to share
and always try to be kind and fair.
I wish to console all the tender heart
absorb and gain all knowledge to impart.
I have imbibed their enthusiasm all through the years,
And when they have questions I am all ears.
They have taught and loved me so much each day,
That I have made teaching my passion all the way.
I want to see my students grow,
and my blessings are always there, they know.

4. MY MOM MY STRENGTH

I look up to the way she listens
and supports me all through the years.
For teaching me to stay strong
and sharing my triumphs and tears.
Her values make me rich and strong
that keeps me protected all along.
She taught me to believe in myself
and always treats me before her self.
Her strong will is my anchor,
and her experiences are my manual.
No hurdle in her difficult life sank her.
Her power and actions I can resonate across.
There ought to be a Hall of Fame for Moms
May heaven help us always remember,
That the hand that the cradle rocks
will always rule the world like an ember.
I couldn't ask for a better mom,
Even in her flaws I see her perfection.
I endeavor her councils to dissipate the darkness,
That helps me to think over my predilection.
Her arms around me are most comforting.
She influences me in the journey of my success,

and empowers me to keep dreaming
and follow them in a way no one can suppress.

5. GROWING WISER

Growing older is a process..
where you become the person
you always should have been.
Days slip in to weeks,
weeks turn into months,
months transform into years,
and you lose your teen.
Calendars are changing and so am I.
Sometimes I find myself acting wisely
and sometimes I just go crazy.
On certain issues I speak vociferously
and at others I just shrug and remain silent.
Situations are changing and so am I.
I have stopped bargaining with the poor vendors,
I pay the auto driver and walk away
without waiting for the change,
to see a smile on their tired face.
Emotions are changing and so am I.
I have learned not to be embarrassed
by my emotions as it makes me human.
After loving my parents, my siblings,
my spouse and my children,
Now I have started loving myself.
Life is becoming good and so am I.

I don't bother about my creased shirt
Or worry about my mismatched dupatta.
I don't bother if my eyebrows are not done
Or think whether fine lines are showing.
Beauty is inside out and so am I.
I have learned to drop the ego
than to break a relationship.
I demand for what is due to me
and stop accepting injustice.
The times are changing and so am I
I'm learning not to let others
make me feel incompetent.
I walk away from people
who never ever value me.
Attitudes are changing and so am I.
I have learned to live each day
as it were the last.
I do what makes me happy
as I owe it to me.
Soul is eternal and so am I.
I have learned not to correct people,
even when I know they are wrong.
I give compliments generously
as freethinking is a mood enhancer.
Peace is precious and so am I.
Yes, I am growing WISER !

6. I WISH.....

I wish to dwell in a world
where people live in ultimate harmony.
Where all the denizens are happy and free,
and our tests are transformed into testimony.
I wish to dwell in a world
where everything is nice and good.
Where characters are honest and sincere
and everyone is dearly understood.
I wish to dwell in a world
where sovereignty and secularism is anthem.
Where peace and tranquility rules us
and mind possess the ability to cope fathom.

7. ARACHNOPHOBIA

Phobias hit almost all of us
that causes great anxiety and distress.
The greatest fear I have of all
is the creepy legs of spiders on the wall.
Panic creates and I start with prep,
when the spider detaches from its web.
Its sight gives me hell of a scare,
when they run in all directions everywhere.
People say I should not create a fuss
as spiders are small compared to us.
But their presence is something I can't bear
and it's crawling triggers a lot of fear.
The phobia is so much there in my head
That I would do anything to get them dead.
Someone help me to stop them from haunting me
and allow me to be peaceful and let me be.

8. ADAM'S ALE

Mind is like water.
When agitated it's difficult to see what lies beneath.
Sometimes we find ourselves in troubled waters,
But may not be to drown but only to be cleansed.
We never know the worth of water
till the well is completely dry.
Likewise men should not lose hope
And never leave without a try.
Even the smallest act of kindness for the cripples
is like a drop of water in the pond
creating a lot of ripples.
Water gives us a sense
of peace and serenity,
which helps us discover
a mindful of clarity.
The rush of a flowing water,
The noise of a crashing wave
and all inspiring water scene,
has always enthralled us naïve.
Spending time in water has
tremendous soothing effects to relate.
As it is reminiscent of time
that transports us to meditative state.

9. MIGHTY NIGHT

All the elders and wise often say,
"After every night there is a brighter day."
As fate whispers to the warrior in me,
"You cannot withstand the storm".
And I being strong willed
whisper back ,"Don't test my inner storm".
Hope and faith during the dark nights
restores my optimism and belief,
That enables me to fight back
the enormous burdens without grief.
The stare that is returned back
when I look at my reflection in mirror.
It compels me to move forward in life
and reject the impulses of error.
Even the longest night
won't last long forever,
And my plans and dreams will
surely come together.

10. SMILE

When you are sad
and feeling very bad,
And someone gives you a smile
How do you feel for a while?
You think the whole world is against you,
But there is someone who really cares for you.
If not ,there is a sweet little smile,
that will be your companion throughout your life.
When the sky is dark,
and sadly sings the lark.
And someone smiles at you,
doesn't the sky turn from black to blue?

11. READING GIVES YOU WINGS

The wisest relation can be with a book
that's a complete exercise for the mind.
Reading is the easiest get-away for a reader
that makes a leader you can find.
Books train your imagination
that you hold today in your hand.
It lifts up your enthusiasm
and takes you to an adventure land.
Try to acquire the habit of reading
and construct a meaningful life.
It will lead you to success
and give you refuge from miseries of life.
Books give wings to the mind
to reach soaring heights, my son.
With knowledge much more refined
will help you broaden your horizon.

12. FAMILY WEDDING

Wedding is a ceremony -
where two individuals are united in marriage.
But when it's a cousin's wedding,
the scenario is to encourage.
It's energetic and romcom full of passion.
The event is more like a festival
with all the cousins in fashion.
The family dynamics are interesting and sweet,
And a family wedding is a luscious celebration
that no one can beat.
The extravagant wedding with gorgeous outfit,
showcases our culture possessing indomitable spirit.
The enormous events are planned
for months at stretch,
Where celebrations last longer
than seasons can fetch.
The entire family gathers
together to have much fun.
Young and old in jovial mood
swing to dance numbers to stun.
Event company look into everything,
With personalized taste and aura.
Starting from the décor
till the function wind up the era.

Much focus is on creating
a phenomenal exexperience.
Effort and money is put into
elaborate events with elegance.
The food served on a platter
stimulate the appetite.
The menu of the wedding
is definitely a treat for the eyes.
Another poignant pleasure is
the gift thats personalized and packed,
And given as a token of appreciation
to the members nicely wrapped.
After attending such a wedding
one's thought surmounts,
It's not the years in your life
but the life in your years that counts.

13. PISCEAN

Pisces people are emotionally sensitive
and regarded as the most sympathetic.
They will go miles to remain energetic
And they are creative and imaginative.
Piscean loves to be surrounded by passionate
and guarded about their personal space.
For them empathy makes for a special place
and look for anchor if they need a soulmate.
Piscean is thought to be the rarest zodiac.
They hate ultimatums and threats,
but are often the cause of their own regret.
They feel things intensely to make a comeback.
Pisceans are extremely intuitive and intelligent,
Their sensitivity is their utmost strength.
They crave for all the attention and care,
They have an optimistic effect that's rare.
Pisceans are extremely sincere and loyal,
Their eyes let you know how they feel.
They readily apologize if they fail,
and avoid conflicts to remain a jovial.

14. WORKING IN A SCHOOL

Working in a school is fulfilling,
where along with work competition is exciting.
Helping students reach their potential
to see that struggling students become successful.
Working in a school is the most satisfying,
Being part of the growth is quite rewarding.
Gives opportunities to build profound relationship,
learning makes school a place of worship.
Working in a school nourishes the mind,
playing a significant role is well defined.
The privilege of making an impact on society
enriched with knowledge and taking away anxiety.
Working in a school gives exposure to development,
Mentoring for academic goal is an enlightenment.
Results demonstrate a substantial association,
That enhances the status of a teaching profession.

15. TRUE RELATIONS

A true relationship
does not happen overnight.
Relationships are strange
that can take you to any height.
Suspicious minds can't build it.
Constant pessimist remarks ruin it.
Being curious rather than furious
will make the situations less serious.
The antidote for becoming defensive
is to find something attentive.
Your sacrifices should not go unnoticed,
or else you would be termed an anecdotist.
Willingness to help in difficulties
and readiness to shoulder responsibility,
will always pave way for
a better understanding with compatibility.

16. GREENERY

Greenery promotes good health,
which improves the quality of human wealth.
Trees are instrumental in purifying air,
and also helps in pacifying despair.
I am in love with the nature's beauty,
that envelops me with its abundant bounty.
As Mother Nature waves her magic wand,
I take pride in her beauty that's grand.
The green leaves adorn my house,
which lets all my anger to douse.
To satiate my hunger for plants,
I often take a stroll in the parks.
I see buildings with green balconies around.
People still grow plants without the ground.
The numerous shades of green
bring a lot of inner sheen.

17. WRATH

The intensity of anger,
can range from profound
annoyance to extremely unsound
situation that identifies with ember.
Anger occurs due to various reasons,
that can be caused by depression
or memories of traumatic expression
that makes a person change like seasons.
Anger is a mental health condition,
where everyone has their own trigger
which makes one quiver
but can be controlled by self admission.
Don't ignore an angry person,
Instead listen to what they have to say.
Make them sit with whom they obey
and never let the situation worsen.

18. SUCCESS

One does not become successful,
by meeting an arbitrary standard.
Elements that make one successful,
is the hard work ,dedication and the set goal.
Strive towards something bigger than yourself,
achieve the knowledge to gratify thyself.
Keep away from all the distractions,
and overcome all obstacles with determination.
Being a successful human is the
ultimate goal of every individual.
Self-confidence is a major factor
that was even followed by the aboriginal.

19. HARMONY

Freedom of religion means
we are secular.
We are diverse
and that makes us peculiar.
All scriptures guide us
to the right path.
Then why do certain elements
go for bloodbath?
Islam means peace acquired
by submitting your will to God.
Love and peace are central
in Christian theme to plod.
Compassion holds an important position
in the teachings of Buddhism.
The whole world is a family,
is a cardinal principle of Hinduism.
Differences in beliefs should not hinder
the progress of people for World Peace.
We should work together in harmony
in the true spirit of service.
Friendly coexistence is
the need of the hour.
Avoid everything that
leaves a scar.

Religious harmony is the most
valuable treasure of India.
Now to uphold this value
is the responsibility of the media.

20. WORDS OF WISDOM

Live humbly,
no matter how wealthy you are.
Keep loving your friends,
no matter how angry you are.
Forgive all,
no matter how hard it is.
Ask for God's forgiveness,
No matter ho big your sin is.
Keep trying hard,
no matter how many times you fail.
Keep believing in yourself,
no matter what people say.
Don't stress yourself,
no matter how bad the situation is.
Think positively,
no matter how bad life treats.
Stay rooted,
no matter where you come from.
Give up things,
no matter how much it weighs you down.
Hate no one,
no matter how they have wronged you.
Never stop praying,
no matter how things have broken you.

Printed by Libri Plureos GmbH in Hamburg,
Germany